SandCastle™

Baby Mammals

It's a Baby Moose!

Kelly Doudna

Consulting Editor, Diane Craig, M.A./Reading Specialist

Published by ABDO Publishing Company, 8000 West 78th Street, Edina, Minnesota 55439.

Copyright © 2008 by Abdo Consulting Group, Inc. International copyrights reserved in all countries.

No part of this book may be reproduced in any form without written permission from the publisher. SandCastle™ is a trademark and logo of ABDO Publishing Company.

Printed in the United States.

Editor: Pam Price
Content Developer: Nancy Tuminelly
Cover and Interior Design and Production: Mighty Media
Photo Credits: Alaska Stock.com, Creatas, Peter Arnold Inc. (R. Frank, Patrick Frischknecht, Chlaus Lotscher, Thomas D. Mangelsen, L. Weyers, U. & M. Wiede), ShutterStock

Library of Congress Cataloging-in-Publication Data

Doudna, Kelly, 1963-
  It's a baby moose! / Kelly Doudna.
    p. cm. -- (Baby mammals)
  ISBN 978-1-60453-026-1
  1. Moose--Infancy--Juvenile literature. I. Title.

QL737.U55D67 2008
599.65'7139--dc22
                    2007036932

SandCastle™ Level: Fluent

SandCastle™ books are created by a team of professional educators, reading specialists, and content developers around five essential components—phonemic awareness, phonics, vocabulary, text comprehension, and fluency—to assist young readers as they develop reading skills and strategies and increase their general knowledge. All books are written, reviewed, and leveled for guided reading, early reading intervention, and Accelerated Reader® programs for use in shared, guided, and independent reading and writing activities to support a balanced approach to literacy instruction. The SandCastle™ series has four levels that correspond to early literacy development. The levels are provided to help teachers and parents select appropriate books for young readers.

| **Emerging Readers** | **Beginning Readers** | **Transitional Readers** | **Fluent Readers** |
| (no flags) | (1 flag) | (2 flags) | (3 flags) |

SandCastle™ would like to hear from you. Please send us your comments and suggestions.
sandcastle@abdopublishing.com

Vital Statistics

for the Moose

BABY NAME
calf

NUMBER IN LITTER
1 to 2, average 1

WEIGHT AT BIRTH
30 pounds

AGE OF INDEPENDENCE
1 year

ADULT WEIGHT
800 to 1,600 pounds

LIFE EXPECTANCY
8 to 15 years

Moose are the largest members of the deer family. A female moose is called a cow. A male moose is a bull.

Moose cows usually give birth to one calf. But sometimes they have twins.

Moose calves gain weight faster than any

Although deer and moose are related, they are not the same. Most baby deer have white spots. But moose calves do not have any spots.

Moose calves communicate by grunting when they are first born. Soon they develop a wail that sounds almost human.

Moose are herbivores. Their diet includes the tender shoots of willow and aspen trees. They also eat water plants such as lilies.

Moose spend most of their time eating

Adult moose defend themselves against predators by kicking with their large hooves. But bears and wolves prey on moose calves.

Moose are very good swimmers. Moose go into water to find food and to escape flies in summer.

Moose can dive as

Young bull moose grow small antlers when they are just one year old.

Moose calves stay with their mothers for one year. When cows have new calves, they drive their older offspring away.

Fun Fact
About the Moose

A bull moose's antlers might span six feet.
That's a wide enough space for a person to fit into!

6 FEET

Glossary

communicate – to share ideas, information, or feelings.

defend – to protect from harm or attack.

expectancy – an expected or likely amount.

herbivore – an animal that eats mainly plants.

independence – the state of no longer needing others to care for or support you.

offspring – the baby or babies of an animal.

predator – an animal that hunts others.

shoot – new plant growth.

span – to reach or extend from one point to another.

wail – a long cry of sadness or pain.

To see a complete list of SandCastle™ books and other nonfiction titles from ABDO Publishing Company, visit **www.abdopublishing.com**.
8000 West 78th Street, Edina, MN 55439
800-800-1312 • 952-831-1632 fax